Going for the Gold: Alchemy in Coaching

Mary R. Bast, Ph.D.

CONTENTS

GOING FOR THE GOLD

Our collective predicament depends much on individual human transformation and we cannot afford not arousing the potential and motivation of individuals to work on themselves to the extent that they can. Claudio Naranjo, "Suggestions for Further Work on Self," *Character and Neurosis.*

In 2009 I viewed Xue Shen and Hongbo Zhao's graceful and Olympic gold-winning pairs skating performance. "This is our fourth Olympics," noted Shen. "We made a comeback to give it our last shot at gold. Words cannot describe how I feel right now. I just want to cry. It is a dream."

Then a friend linked me to a video of another Chinese pair in a "she without arm, he without leg" ballet, whose profoundly moving performance changed the meaning for me of "going for the gold."

In coaching we have the privilege of witnessing both kinds of *gold*. During my first few years as an executive coach, I was more focused on Olympian goals with my clients, who achieved their promotions, managed their teams for higher morale and productivity, or—in the bronze medal category of coaching—reinstated themselves instead of being fired.

With some, however, my simply being present and mirroring encouraged much more, so I began to look for ways to reframe "going for the gold" in coaching. This is not about winning, not about being right, more caring, confident, unique, smart, inventive, strong, or content, but about a greater illumination.

Do we have the right to challenge clients to transformational work when they've asked only for help with their leadership or communication skills, or similar behavioral goals? Deep change—as indicated by these alchemical metaphors—is disorienting, discomfiting, and even frightening.

Nonetheless, I believe it is our Great Work to be courageous enough to go for the gold. Of course, not every client is ready or wants to make the leap great coaching demands, but those who do find far more rewards than they could have anticipated when they started out to resolve an immediate problem.

Alchemy may seem a grandiose metaphor for this awakening, but alchemists believe everything will become more advanced given time; the "Great Work" is simply to speed up that process.

So why not imagine our Great Work is to help accelerate our clients' transformation? Now envision the Enneagram as a dynamic vessel within which alchemical processes take place.

Below are nine elements of alchemy, arranged in numerical sequence so you can see the Enneagram parallels. Also keep in mind that each element, rather than being unique to an Enneagram style, is vital to the transformation process in all nine:

Calcinatio—purifying by fire subjects the basic material to intense heat, driving away alien substances and leaving a pure, whitened ash. Psychologically speaking, this works on the mind and ego, burning away the false self. The whitened ash represents release from our personality's fixated illusion of reality.

Solutio—melting hard hearts and entrenched positions uses the purifying and dissolving properties of water to return the ash to its most basic state so it can be worked with successfully. This dissolution works on the heart to release buried emotions.

Solificatio—making things real, represents moving from the lower to the higher mind. Our deep intention to change is not limited by rational thought and conscious goal attainment, but rather our thoughts are *enlightened*, transformed into light, a vision of what is possible.

Nigredo—separating the extraneous from the real. This aspect of alchemy means putrefaction or decomposition, all ingredients cleansed and cooked to a uniform black matter, representing the moment of maximum despair, the dark night of the soul, the dying of inner chaos and doubt, discovering what really matters, what is authentic essence.

Separatio—separating wholes into components, separating the essence of dissolution from its wastes. This refers to *dismembering* the personality, retrieving the energy released by dissolution of negative beliefs and emotional blockages.

Mortificatio—killing or dead-making, consciously working on reduction of ego attachments; in Jungian terms going inside ourselves to embrace the shadow so our self reflects the whole instead of a dissociated part.

Sublimatio—infusing with spirit, transmuting to a higher form. In chemistry a solid, when heated, passes directly into gas and ascends to the top of the vessel, where it resolidifies. Metaphorically we are made spiritual, we move *above* and see objectively.

Coagulatio—mastering the forces of nature, accessing our own soul power to change our reality on all levels. This refers to earth and to being solid, to a chemical reaction that produces a new compound. In *coagulatio* we seek stability with our newfound peace and become accustomed to our spirit-based self.

Coniunctio—uniting apparent opposites to make a larger whole. Here we unite conscious/unconscious, balance masculine/feminine principles, increase intuitive insights/ synchronicities, and enter psychological wholeness.

To join the mystery with clients entering the crucible, we, too, must prepare, asking "How can my presence as a coach help them step into the fire, free buried and repressed emotions, discover and pursue an illuminated vision, hold to the course when shaken by disorientation or despair, dissolve negative beliefs, *kill* their ego attachments, find a new spiritual perspective and soul power, and become more whole?"

CALCINATIO:
LETTING GO AN ILLUSION OF REALITY

Calcinatio, purifying by fire, is the first of the alchemy procedures, subjecting the basic material to intense heat, driving away alien substances and leaving a pure, whitened ash. Psychologically, this is the burning away of the false self. The whitened ash represents release from our personality's fixated illusion of reality.

Whenever we are consumed by raging anger, this is the ego's habitual response to feeling threatened. In *The Nine Ways of Working*, Michael Goldberg uses the *calcinatio* metaphor with Ones, "fire-breathing dragons with very good manners. Their dragon fire can be a sanctifying, purifying fire – something to test your mettle and make you the best you can be – or it can be a punishing hellfire that will burn you to a crisp."

However, when we're angry and learn to stay *with* the fire, not reacting, not obsessing over how and who to burn to a crisp, we let the anger *go to ground*, finding and releasing the illusion that everyone *should* behave a certain way and it's our job to *fix* them.

Here's how Jan, Enneagram Style One, describes changes she's experienced:

I used to have the sense "If I don't flog it and work really hard at it, it won't be enough." I became aware of a pattern where a grievance with someone in a work situation would give me an excuse to get angry.

My story was "Unless I'm right and good I cannot love or be loved," and that's not true, of course.

Since then I've learned ways to release anger so I don't devastate the countryside, no one dies, and no tragedy occurs. I've come to allow the lid to rest a little more lightly on the pot. I'm not pushing it down so hard for fear the contents will explode. I'm more in touch with my anger, aware when it comes up, and find new ways to express it, often in creative efforts.

This burning through releases creative energy, passion, and grounded idealism that can change the world.

SOLUTIO:
RELEASING BURIED EMOTIONS

Solutio uses the purifying and dissolving properties of water to return to its most basic state the whitened ash left from burning away our ego-based illusion of reality. This dissolution works on the heart to release buried emotions.

Some people find it particularly difficult to acknowledge and explore their own needs and emotions. All of us, though, have elements of self-image fed by pride that form barriers to self-knowledge.

As my Style Two client Doris said:

It's been tough for me in the journey to discover behaviors I don't like about myself. It was relatively easy to take a serious step away from trying to fix the lives of everyone around me.

The hard part is taking charge of my own life, loving and accepting myself and other people for who we are, and it's O.K. if I'm screwed up.

The way I'm most different is with my daughter. I used to fix everything because I didn't want her to hurt, I didn't want her or her kids to do without. I enabled her to avoid reality, and I've not done her a service.

So I've gently eased out of that, though it was a struggle. She'd say, "Mom, my daughter forgot this, can you run it by her school," and I learned to say, "No, honey, I'm sorry, I'm late for work."

If something comes in my face a couple of times and I think I've dealt with it, but it keeps coming back, I know I haven't dealt with it!

I've used journaling and meditating to help me get a clean slate, stay centered. It's a journey and I know I'll slip off the path, but not quite as deep anymore.

Being able to recognize these patterns when they come up has been such a gift. I always know that no matter what happens, I'll get through it.

SOLIFICATIO:
A VISION OF THE POSSIBLE

Solificatio, making things real, represents moving from the lower to the higher mind. Our deep intention to change is not limited by rational thought and conscious goal attainment, but rather our thoughts are "enlightened," literally transformed into light, a vision of what is possible.

A key aspect of going beyond apparent needs is realizing how we've been driven by unconscious patterns, pushing us toward goals that satisfy an ego-image, not our highest potential.

Solificatio symbolizes helping our clients envision what's possible beyond materialistic aspirations. Tom's path as a Style Three demonstrates moving beyond the image of *looking good*:

All my life, until I started doing some real work on myself, it was "how things look" as opposed to how I really am. I was living a lie: "How do I fool people?" I wasn't conscious of it, but my image, how people saw me, was more important than anything.

I was a football and baseball coach early in my career, and I got a really choice spot in a choice school. Being a sports coach might be altruistic in helping students achieve something, but the raw motivation was to be out there in front – to get noticed, to have people say, "Oh, just look at him! He's a great guy!"

It was exciting, challenging, frustrating. I loved being a leader, putting my ideas into practice. It was also an area where I could have self-doubt and pretend I didn't.

I got the conflicting message as a child that I was supposed to be good enough and smart enough to become a doctor, a lawyer, or some other professional, while something in me longed to play music at a very early age. My parents discouraged me from studying a musical instrument because

9

"they'd spend money on lessons and I wouldn't be good enough and would quit."

I did later sing and perform, initially to move through some of those inhibitions, and then I created a whole work around it for others, teaching them to feel the fear and do it anyway... to move through and let the experience teach you something different from what's in your head.

I still might look good to others, but I'm getting away from the image of looking good, and just doing what I love to do.

At 61 I'm also moving into community work, volunteer efforts, and this feels good and right. When I was focused on how I looked to others I was pretty much of a loner, but more and more I really enjoy sharing and working with others.

NIGREDO:
THE DARKNESS BEFORE THE DAWN

Nigredo—separating the extraneous from the real. This aspect of alchemy means putrefaction or decomposition, all ingredients cleansed and cooked to a uniform black matter, representing the moment of maximum despair, the dark night of the soul, the dying of inner chaos and doubt, discovering what really matters, what is authentic essence.

On my first long car trip with a new GPS, I felt I had my personal traffic controller, especially as the sun began to set and I couldn't see the road signs to my son's apartment in an unfamiliar city. What a relief, when driving in the dark, to hear a voice saying "in 100 feet, turn right."

Without a map or GPS when seeking a new destination, our tendency is to either succumb to panic or turn back to more familiar roads. Likewise, the journey of transformation is not rational or linear, there is certainly no GPS, and it can take heroic effort to stay present and open to the change.

Carolyn Myss calls this *spiritual madness*. When we help our clients stay centered and endure the *madness*, they begin to hear their internal GPS, their own voice of guidance. And Myss endearingly adds, "How do you expect the answer to be given to you? It's not going to come in a letter!"

Nora, Style Four, describes her emerging voice of guidance:

> *I think in the process of our evolution we have things that block us. Leonard Laskow speaks of "treasured wounds" and beliefs. So for me the exploration is seeing how I've held things that kept me from moving forward.*

> *One of my core issues has been not feeling I'm good enough. Early on I had so little sense of myself that I'd go away in my head. Many of my struggles were in learning to get past that, to stay in real time, to stay in the midst of whatever was*

scaring me, which was usually a threat proving there was something terribly wrong with me. I have the image that along the way you move from pain and toward possibilities.

There have been a number of lessons for me. One is to trust that what and where I am right now, without any exaggeration or drama, is enough. Another is that life without drama isn't mediocre or bland, it's living from the center. It wasn't the events or people in my life, it was the emotional energy I gave to them that was the problem. Drama pulled me away from my heart.

SEPARATIO:
DISSOLVING NEGATIVE BELIEFS AND EMOTIONAL BLOCKAGES

Separatio, separating wholes into components, separating the essence of dissolution from its wastes. This refers to "dismembering" the personality, retrieving the energy released by dissolution of negative beliefs and emotional blockages.

In *Thoughts Without a Thinker* Mark Epstein shares an encounter between a Zen master and Kalu Rinpoche, a Tibetan monk. This was intended to be dharma combat, the clashing of great minds.

The Zen master, obviously ready to parry any response, held up an orange and asked repeatedly "What is this?" "What is this?"

After several moments of silence, the Tibetan whispered to the monk beside him, who then translated: "Rinpoche says, 'What is the matter with him? Don't they have oranges where he comes from?'"

Some people rely on intellect to make sense of the world and their existence in it. It's important as a coach to meet them where they are, inviting them to question their own assumptions, but without being drawn into dharma combat.

For example, John, an Enneagram Five, began our work together with intellectual fervor, clearly articulating his desire to "become aware of my assumptions, biases, and limitation and begin consciously choosing different assumptions and points of view."

Notice, in his self-description below, how John first had to access his beliefs through intellectual awareness, and only gradually became aware of his emotions:

A deep interest in Jung came in realizing this was a fascinating way to understand myself and others. Jungians say you need to have some contact with your unconscious to develop the axis between your ego and your inner core.

Having a mental framework has legitimized it for me. I like the whole intellectual idea that we've been living in some kind of unconscious activity, and we try to get out of being "asleep."

When my marriage ended it was a blow to my self-esteem. Specifically, I realized I didn't understand what feelings were all about. My wife accused me of not having feelings, of being too logical, and I didn't know what she was talking about.

Finally, I realized intellectually I needed to do something, and that's when I sought help. I had to accept all this horrible unconscious stuff, and finally realized I really did have feelings. I realized I was just thinking too much.

Now I reveal more when I'm comfortable with someone, noting, for example, "I'm probably too much in my head right now."

MORTIFICATIO:
KILLING EGO ATTACHMENTS

Mortificatio—killing or dead-making, consciously working on reduction of ego attachments; in Jungian terms 'bringing home' our projections, going inside ourselves to embrace the shadow so our being reflects the whole instead of a dissociated part.

Before I knew anything about *mortificatio,* I thought only of "mortification," as in *humiliation* or *shame*—feelings most of us prefer to avoid. But perhaps that's the point.

Humiliation and shame are ego-responses. And a counselor or coach can unwittingly reinforce the notion that unwanted behavior is "bad" by suggesting ways to *stop* doing what clients *don't like* about their behavior.

Instead, we can show them how to be *with,* to embrace these unwanted aspects. Paradoxically, they can then find their authentic selves.

Enneagram style Six, David had a late and rapid change in his life at age 60:

> *Frankly, when I first looked at your web site I thought, "My god, this is some sort of cult!" Later, I realized that same skepticism and fear had kept me from the very change I'd longed for, had – in fact – been a hallmark in my career.*
>
> *I didn't trust many people. This often showed up as anger and it cost me an expected promotion to President of our company. The CEO said, "You know, I'm worried about you; you're angry and accusing beyond anything that's called for."*
>
> *I'd fight to the death to defend a position and at the same time carry tremendous guilt that I either turned people off with my complaining or scared them away.*

What's so awesome to me is that I have absolute, unqualified trust in this process. I marvel that I'd gone through life always having to know where I was going, figuring out everything that could possibly go wrong; otherwise I wasn't going to do it.

Now it's joy that moves me through the process and I don't care where it ends. I've tossed the road map.

SUBLIMATIO:
INFUSING WITH SPIRIT

Sublimatio—In the chemical process of sublimation, a heated solid enters a gaseous state and ascends to the cooler top of the vessel where it re-solidifies. Thus in alchemical lore, sublimatio symbolizes transmuting to a higher form. Metaphorically, we become more spiritual, we move "above" our small ego-types and have a larger worldview.

For many years I've been amused by Charles Tart's coined word, *endarkenment.* Tart, an icon of spiritual consciousness, wrote "A way to get endarkened really well is to be narrow, to only see things one way."

I've experienced occasional shifts to higher stages of consciousness as stepping out of the dark and into the light. But Tart's somewhat tongue-in-cheek admission, "My specialty is endarkenment," reflects how occasional those glimpses of light can be.

One of my Enneagram Seven clients described this larger worldview as a *mosaic.* "It's not like the old disappears, but the pieces can be put together in infinite combination."

Below is a brief recap of her particular endarkenment—to put a positive spin on things and ignore reality—as well as one glimpse of light in her mosaic:

> *I grew up in a family like the one in Ordinary People, where everything looked good on the outside. My parents were upper-middle-class, church-going, and provided for all our needs, but emotionally there was chaos and conflict.*
>
> *My friends would say, "I wish I had your parents," and I'd think, "How could that be?" That was exaggerated: in college "Gosh, how is it that everyone else seems to know what's going on and says it's OK, but it doesn't feel OK to me?"*

I spent my last semester of college in Mexico studying Latin American history and politics, and stayed two weeks with a family where there were only two beds and only two rooms with paved floors.

I became aware not only how my family pretended everything was OK, but that in the U.S. everyone else looked that way, too. Now I was with people who didn't live that way at all.

That's continued to be a reminder to me. When I'm feeling out of my element, instead of running away from reality or trying to put a spin on it, to embrace it and ask, "Well, if I were in Mexico, what would I do?"

COAGULATIO:
BECOMING SOMEBODY AND NOBODY

*Coagulatio—is the process that turns something into earth...
The churn of reality solidifies the personality... it has become
attached to an ego. In Jungian terms, coagulatio symbolizes
the fulfillment of individuation, to be followed by other
alchemical processes. "What has become fully concretized is
now subject to transformation." (Edward F. Edinger in
Anatomy of the Psyche)*

In *Paths Beyond Ego* John H. Engler wrote, "The therapeutic
issue in psychotherapy... is to 're-grow' a basic sense of self"
whereas "the therapeutic issue in Buddhism is how to 'see
through' the illusion or construct of the self." The two goals are
not mutually exclusive. Rather, there is a wider perspective
where they are compatible: "Put very simply, you have to be
somebody before you can be nobody."

Reading Engler's essay gave me an "aha" moment. I'd been
wrestling with some differences among clients in how they
express their experience of transformational change.

Some describe becoming more sure of themselves, which can
seem a strengthening of their ego-image, yet they are clearly
also shifting to greater self-awareness.

Others refer to an awareness of self from the perspective of an
objective witness, seeing how programmed and habitual ego
responses have operated.

Realizing both are necessary has helped me understand the
symbolism of *coagulatio*. We have to become *somebody* before
we can be *nobody*.

Thus my Style Eight client, Bart, until his fifties, had been
consolidating himself as a strong and fearless man. He had to
become himself fully, to individuate, to operate in the world
without apology, knowing he was just fine as he was. Only then

could he begin to step out into a broader perspective, one where he saw through the illusion of needing to be strong and could begin the path to becoming *nobody*:

> *I had a long history of seeking adrenaline rushes. I was keen on river rafting and I wanted to do it in wild rivers like the Amazon, rivers you could gauge by the number of maimings they have per season.*
>
> *Then I was hit by a truck and broke several ribs and an arm, with some nerve damage.*
>
> *It was distressing that I was now only as strong as a regular person and forced to ask for help in ways I never had before. I had always tended to approach every act as a Warrior with absolutely everything he's got. Being partially incapacitated, I learned how tied I'd been to the need to be strong.*
>
> *I often think of the loss, both to me and all the people who knew me before this change. I was always back in the cave, conjecturing, ready to take a pot-shot, and I would never share.*
>
> *Now, when I'm really listening to someone, it's like walking down the sidewalk with our arms around each other, in step, making eye contact, walking together.*

CONIUNCTIO:
ACCESSING POLARITIES, BECOMING WHOLE

> *Coniunctio—bringing together apparent opposites to make a larger whole; for example, uniting conscious and unconscious, balancing masculine and feminine principles, incorporating extroversion and introversion and, later, entering psychological wholeness.*

In *Anatomy of the Psyche,* Edward F. Edinger describes alchemical operations as "basic categories by which to understand the life of the psyche" which "illustrate almost the full range of experiences that constitute individuation." He adds that many of the alchemical images overlap, and echoes the Jungian belief that there's no prescribed sequence.

It's also been my experience that each person I coach has to undergo all alchemical processes, and not necessarily in the same order as others. So the order I've presented is arbitrary. More important, none of the client examples is meant to convey greater or lesser aspects of significant change; only *different* aspects.

Coniunctio may seem in its definition to represent a culmination of all the operations. It's important to understand, however, that this symbol includes two processes, first the bringing together of apparent opposites ("the lesser *coniunctio*"), and then later the *union* of the opposites, which is greater than the sum of its parts ("the greater *coniunctio* combines the opposites, mitigates and rectifies all one-sidedness").

So balancing masculine and feminine, for example, is not "a little of this, a little of that." In the case of the Enneagram Nine client quoted below, her efforts to become more assertive did not lead to wholeness as long as she was still polarized between anxiety and confidence. The two kinds of change she describes represent her experience of the "lesser" and the "greater" *coniunctio*:

I've experienced two kinds of change in my life. The first is not a major shift but rather becoming more effective at what I've always done. For example, when I was in graduate school I was so nervous presenting papers in class, I wished the earth would open up and swallow me. So I took assertiveness training and then taught assertiveness courses myself. I learned the behaviors that helped me act less nervous in front of a group.

I think of that as incremental change. I hadn't changed inside, but knew how to handle anxiety when it appeared. I still felt a polarity between keeping quiet and girding myself up to speak in public.

The second kind of change is much more significant, a bolt of lightning where I suddenly "get" something about myself, a shift from being asleep to awakening.

Relative to assertiveness, I "got" that behind the anxiety was a child who believed nobody was interested in what she had to say. When I allowed myself to experience that child and her story fully, something fundamental shifted inside.

The story no longer matters. There is no polarity. I am both quiet and outspoken, both soft and strong.

ABOUT THE AUTHOR

Mary Bast is a coach and coach mentor who works by phone with clients worldwide.

Author of *Somebody? Nobody? The Enneagram, Mindfulness and Life's Unfolding*; *Out of the Box: Coaching with the Enneagram*; *Out of the Box Self-Coaching Workbook*; *Out of the Box Coaching Field Guide*; and *Buddhism & the Enneagram*, Mary is also a painter and writes poetry and memoir.

Out of the Box Coaching: http://www.breakoutofthebox.com
Coach Mentor: http://mentoringforcoaches.blogspot.com
Self-Coaching Tips: http://outoftheboxcoaching.blogspot.com
Fine Art: http://www.marybast.com
Poetry/Found Poetry: http://windingsheets.blogspot.com